HOW TO RUN AUDITIONS

A comprehensive guide for film students to
running efficient, effortless auditions.

By Tamar Kummel

ISBN 978-0-6151-4689-8

DEDICATION:

This book is dedicated to you. To all the hard working, day dreaming, starry eyed, bleary eyed, creative souls that are the future of this industry. Keep believing in yourself, and keep making magic for the rest of us.

TABLE OF CONTENTS:

INTRODUCTION

I've been a performer for almost all of my life. I've worked in every aspect of the business: acting, directing, producing, makeup, lights, sets, production assistant, talent agent, casting director and more. I've been to hundred's of auditions over the years and finally I realized that no one was thoroughly teaching film students how to actually run auditions. Film students are taught every other aspect of film making: directing, editing, production. Yet, the audition is critical. The cast will make or break your film. The audition sets the tone for the rest of the production. It's where the actors and director meet for the first time. Actors are taught how to audition for you. Why aren't you taught how to run auditions for them?

Do you want to make a good impression? Do you want to at least appear organized? More importantly, do you want the best actors? Do you want the actors that will be the best to work with? Then this is the book for you.

I have polled hundreds of actors and gotten their pet peeves about auditions, plus their suggestions. I've run plenty of auditions so I've seen them from both sides. I know what the actors are thinking, and I know what you're thinking. Guess what?! It's the same thing. The actor wants to be good and get the role and you want the actor to be good so you can give them the role. But if you are completely clueless at how to have them audition, then you will never know if you cast the best person. You'll just have the last man standing. I want you to have plenty of actors to choose from and attract the best people. I want you to run such an organized, welcoming, friendly audition that every

actor comes out thinking, "That was actually fun! They

were really nice. I want to work with them." What you

DON'T want every actor saying while walking out is,

"They were totally clueless. That was the most

uncomfortable, unorganized, pathetic waste of time. If

the audition is bad, the production could be horrible.

Even if I get it, I won't take it." Right? Let's get

started.

10

GENERAL

These guidelines are best used for student film auditions, but there is a section at the end with suggestions for plays and musical auditions too. I say "student" work, because the more professional you get, the better chance you won't be holding your own initial auditions. However, it's important to understand the process because you will be overseeing the Casting Director's choices of material and actors, and attending the final callbacks.

Remember that you need actors, and they need you. You want and need them to be good and be prepared. They took time off to be there and be ready, so please be respectful and appreciative.

I hate books that generalize how to talk to actors. Actors are not children and they don't like to be treated that way. They are also not crazy people and they especially don't like to be treated that way. Actors are extremely creative, highly intelligent, emotionally complex people. No two are alike. At all. You simply can not communicate the same way with every one, just like you don't explain things to your significant other the same way you talk to your dad. There are hundreds of acting schools and they each have their own language so don't even try to learn "the right way" of talking to an actor. Treat them as people and they will treat you the same way back. More on that later.

Some actors are good at cold readings, some are not. Some are dyslexic. Some are good at improvisation, some are not. Some audition well, but don't perform well. Some perform well, but don't audition well. The idea is to create the best world possible for them so they can do their best, and you can get as accurate an idea as possible of what their acting and personality is like. And yes, their personality is important.

Here's what you want in an actor:

Takes direction well (literally and emotionally)

Plays well with others (literally and emotionally)

Is responsible

Is emotionally available for the demands of the role

Understands the part

Understands the time commitment of the job

Enthusiasm and dedication.

Looks right for the role

Here's what you don't want in an actor:

Doesn't listen to you when you give direction

Isn't able to understand the direction given

Fights against the direction or gives excuses

Is late, obnoxious, unclean, unstable

Is irresponsible and may leave you hanging

Of course, I'm presuming that the actors you
see will be extremely prepared, talented, relaxed and in
top form. That's not always the case. And there are
legitimate reasons why some actors come in extremely
nervous, or not as prepared as they'd hoped, or not as
on time as they wished. But we'll have to assume
together that your audition is a best case scenario and
you're seeing the actors in a generally prepared
situation. I have no control over the actors (that's for
another person's book). But I do have suggestions for
you. It's your audition and you're in control.

BEFORE

So you've decided to produce/direct a film. You need actors. You need to get ready for the audition. What does that mean?

Where do you find actors? Well, it depends on a few things:

Union or non?

Paid or not?

How many roles to fill?

Unique roles to fill?

In or out of town?

Length of time commitment?

There is a list (APPENDIX) at the end of the book of places to list auditions.

No matter what, you want professional actors. You do NOT want your sister/cousin/mom. I know they work cheap and they promised to listen to your suggestions. But they're not trained, they're not as pretty as you think, they won't really listen to you, and most of all-they're not talented. Sorry. It had to be said. You want one of the 100,000's of actors out there that studied hard, cried daily, got in touch with all their mixed up feelings, and want to be in a film. They do have talent, they will listen to you, and they want to be there. They will make or break your production. Trust me. Now, if your brother happens to be a well established actor and you get along harmoniously, cast him. Now.

How do you find actors? You place an ad in Backstage or on theatrical websites (current list in index). You place posters up in your school (if there's an acting department). Many places are free to list. The most important thing in the ad is to list as much information as possible:

Audition date/time/what to prepare

Production and rehearsal dates/times

Union/non-union

Paid/not paid

Casting breakdown (age, sex, special skills, nudity or not*, etc)

Contact info

You want the ad to look professional. So please check that your spelling is correct, that it's in proper English (you'd be surprised), that your email/website link works, etc. Take out physical descriptions of characters unless it's vital. You don't want to rule anyone out. Your view of the character may change. But do give as much information about the character as needed. Example: character will need to feel comfortable with stage combat/nudity/love scenes/singing/dancing/playing piano/improvisation/French accent.

Example of a good ad: Casting Kummel College senior thesis film. SAG student film agreement. Shoot in Upstate NY March 3-10, must be available all dates. Casting 3 roles: MOM: 50 ish, Indian (must be able to do accent), plays tuba. BOB: early 30's, Caucasian, role has nudity. SARA: any ethnicity, 20's, tap dancer. No pay, but transportation, meals, and a copy of finished film. Please submit headshot/resume to Vincent (director/writer) at casting123@email.com. Full script on www.weBfilm.com

That ad is clear, your actors will know exactly what skills they need, when they must be available, who to contact, and what the contract is. And even better, they can read the full script in advance and get an idea about the production company (future company?) from the website.

Example of a bad ad: Casting film. No pay, but as meals. 5 Roles: 20-50. Some have nudity. Send info. To Imanidiot@school.edu

It's unclear the roles, the contract is missing, whether it's union or not, when it's shooting, and there are type-o's. So even if you do get ANY experienced actors sending in headshots to you, ½ will be out of town during the shoot, or wrong for parts, or union when you're not.

It's better to put as much information as you have, than not enough. So if you're not sure of shoot dates, put "Spring" or "April weekends TBA". If you're not shooting in town, but not sure where yet, put, "out of town shoot, transportation provided". And please double check spelling and grammar, especially of your contact information. There's nothing worse than putting the wrong email address.

And if you choose to put your email address only, you better have a large account that can handle giant files and check it constantly. You may easily get 100 emails the first day.

To be union or not?

If you want your production to be as good as possible, with the best people and the most chance of success, then you want it to be union. Most schools have an agreement with SAG/AEA for students.

Although it does require more paperwork, it's still the

best option. Get it. Use it. Call the unions if you have

questions. Someday you're going to want to be well

established in their conclave. Start now.

There is always the temptation to go non-union.

If you have NO money then I understand wanting to

work non-union. It's cheaper and easier, yes. But

you'll be using people with less experience. If you're

mounting a stage production, only non-union theaters

(less respected, less clean, less accessible) will be

available for you. And you'll have no resources at your

disposal. The unions have rules about how actors and

crew need to be treated. They're not crazy rules,

they're rules that everyone should follow for every

production. And you may not realize you've been

taking advantage of people until you sign your first

union contract.

Some directors will try to convince union

actors to work in a non-union production. This is

shameless. It's insulting to the actor and all the actors

in the world. They worked hard to become union. The

union protects them from people like that. It has BARE

minimums for pay, food, breaks, etc. You want happy,

healthy actors and crew. You don't want slave labor

unless you are hoping for a coup in the middle of

production. If you want a real career and to not

complete just 1 film/play your entire life, then you

better treat people with the honesty and respect they

deserve. You better learn the correct procedure. At

least try to make it union.

You have several options when it comes to the type of audition.

1)   OPEN CALL: An open call is when you have a big block of time and possibly 200 actors all show up in the same 10 minutes. They get pissed off. You get rushed. And you get overwhelmed trying to see everyone. If 1000 people have shown up, and you have 2 hours to see them all, your only option is to do a "typing out process". This is approximately 5-20 actors in a row standing there while you quickly figure out who you want to keep around. It ranges from an actor saying their name, or singing 8 bars, or doing 1 pirouette, or nothing. It doesn't allow for any flexibility in the casting process, but it does save a lot of time. If only 5 actors show up at your open call, you'll have plenty of time to see them, but no one to

choose from. This could be because established actors usually won't attend open calls.

2)   OPEN CALL/APPOINTMENT COMBO: set up a block of time for an Open Call where appointment times will be given at the door. The actor shows up and signs up for a specific time. This works fine for you, but it's not the best use of actor's time since they may show up at 8:00 AM only to find the next available appointment is at 6:00PM. Also, you may end up with long stretches of no appointments, yet you can't leave because you said you'd be there at certain times.

3)   SUBMISSION OPTION: The best case scenario is to have actors (or agents) submit headshots and resumes (if they don't have them, they're not professional) in advance and then call/email with

appointment times. This gives you the chance to see if an actor will fit a role you're casting before you waste both your times. You also see if an actor shows initiative, is responsible about getting back to you, and has professional headshots, etc. You can do this through email or mail, or through an agent. The drawback with this method is that you may miss seeing someone you wouldn't think would be right for the role, but is actually perfect. Example: You are picturing a tall, skinny blond for a certain role. So you throw out all the short brunette headshots. But if you saw them at an open call, you might find the short brunette that changes your mind about the role. It happens every day. However, this is still the best method because you weed out a lot of actors that are definitely not what you want.

There are pluses and minuses for each method. But you want the best use of time for all involved.

Be sure when setting a schedule that you allow plenty of time with each person. You don't want to be rushed at all. You need to allow time for them to get in/out, say hello (and please do introduce yourself, or at least put a list on the outside of the door saying who's in the room), read each scene/monologue twice, write notes about/discuss them after they leave, and at least 2 minutes to talk to them. That's anywhere from 5-15 minutes a person depending on what you need. Obviously allow more time if there's more you need to see. Also put your lunch breaks (and maybe even bathroom breaks) into the schedule.

You want to be as organized as possible. You need to allow for things to go wrong. The room you rented may not be empty on time. You will have actors show up way before their time slot. Or if you're having an open call, you may have tons of actors showing up hours before the time starts. Make a list of everything you need (see below) and then fill it. Get a professional actor to be a reader. Do not read the scene with the auditioning actor yourself. You want to be able to watch and listen, not react and influence the auditioning actor. Be there early and ready on time. Don't run late. Don't take unscheduled breaks. Be prepared and actors will respect you.

THINGS TO PREPARE:

1. Place casting ads.

2. Pick audition scenes (AKA "sides")/ask for monologues/etc.

3. Get a GOOD reader for the audition

4. Get a professional studio (more on this in a minute)

5. Make audition forms.

6. Create a timeline.

7. Create a sign in sheet.

8. Get someone to monitor.

9. Reserved video camera and person to run it.

Please book a professional studio (or audition room in your school) that has little inside or outside noise. Air conditioning can be noisy. Some studios are better than others. If you rent the right space, every actor will be familiar with it before you give the address. If you rent the wrong space, ½ the actors will be scared to come. Find something clean, well run, in a safe neighborhood, with a waiting area, a tuned piano (if it's a musical audition), and preferably sizable so they're not RIGHT on top of you. Auditions in your apartment can be acceptable if you explain ahead that it will be in your apt, and that you plus 1 or 2 others will be there. This works if your apartment is big enough to have actors wait in a separate room while someone else is auditioning. If it's in your apt, it better look professional and not be in your bedroom. I suggest an internet search (and word of mouth) on local rehearsal studios. Acting schools/theater companies/dance studios/etc. They all have studios for rent.

I had an audition for an independent film. I was told they were seeing union and non-union actors. When I arrived, it turned out to be someone's apartment. There were several people waiting in the living room and the audition was in the bedroom. The living room clearly had been used to store all the furniture they took out of the bedroom. So it looked like a garbage dump. That's what I walked in on. When I got in the tiny bedroom, there were so many people behind the desk, that the row curved around until the person on the end was practically touching me. I read the scene, they asked about my availability, and then suggested that union actors were going to do the film under a different name so that they wouldn't get in trouble with the union. I had just wasted a lot of time submitting, preparing, going to the audition, only to be told that if I did the film I'd be scabbing (going against my union). They should NEVER have seen any union actors and how dare they suggest we lie. Union actors can get in tremendous trouble if they do non-union work and the union finds out. And it's extremely unfair to be asked.

What do you want the actors to prepare? Do you give sides ahead? The whole play/film? Monologues/songs, interview, improvisation, dance, juggle, mime, and other special skills needed?

You have choices. Those choices will depend on how prepared you are. If the script is completed and excellent, I would recommend having the whole thing available for the auditioners to read, preferably before they arrive at the audition. If your script isn't as good as you think, this could backfire on you. But why are you producing a less-than-par script? I suggest at least having scenes for each character emailed/faxed/mailed to the actors WELL IN ADVANCE of their audition (NOT at midnight the night before, and NOT just as they walk in). The more time the actors have with the script, and the more of the script they've read, the better the choices they can make at the audition. That way the actor knows the script is about incest/ rape, has a love scene, the character dies/fires a gun/roller blades, etc. They see how the character fits in the group. If you first hand an actor a script when they arrive at the audition the actor will have to make very quick choices. These choices are not at all necessarily the ones they would make had they had 2 days to prepare.

I recently attended an audition for a film. I did not know for what role I was reading until I arrived. I was then handed 3 different scenes and roles to read. I now had 5 minutes to understand 3 completely different characters! And one character was blind. Obviously, if I'd had a few days more with the script, my reading would have been completely different.

You also can, and should also have plenty of extra copies of the sides at the audition. They should all have clearly marked scenes: BEGINNING/END and for which character at the top of the page.

Give more than one side so there's more to choose from. Each scene should show different emotions or sides of the character. You want to see if the actor has emotional range and understands the character. Be sure to use all the sides, or tell the actor they have a choice. Don't expect all scenes to be prepared the same. Don't ask the actors to prepare more than they will use, and don't ask to show things that were not asked to prepare. Don't waste their time. Be specific. It's a balance of information. Too much is overwhelming and too little is not useful. It may be helpful to write a short synopsis of the film and have it in the audition notice, and also at the audition.

Monologues are OK, but not entirely practical. If you don't have a finished script yet, then a monologue is one option. Suggest they bring in a monologue that compares with your script (contemporary/young/comedy/age range/etc.) But bear in mind that some actors are very good at monologues and some are not. And it doesn't mean they'll be good in your film.

Interviews are helpful, and should be incorporated into any audition. You want to hear them speak, you want to interact, you want to see if they're open, friendly, considerate, enthusiastic, experienced, speak English (or whatever language you need). Just don't put the actor too much on the spot or ask extremely personal questions. And DON'T ask their age. That's not a legal question. If they look right for the part, that's all that matters.

Lastly, there's improvisation. Here's the main question: Do YOU have a background in improvisation? Will you be shooting without a finished script? Will you be shooting in a fashion that allows the actors to play with lines? Then, and only then do I suggest doing improvisation at the audition. If you want your script acted as written, and you've had no instruction yourself then PLEASE don't try to improvise with the actors. They're probably better at it than you are and you're hindering their audition. And you won't learn anything from it. If your script needs to be funnier/better when shooting and you know the writing won't get better, then ask your actors about their background in improvisation.

I had an audition for a student film. They were seeing people over a span of 4 hours. I had an appointment, but I came about an hour early in the hopes of getting done sooner. When I arrived, there was no one there to greet me. There were no sides or audition notices. There were however, 2 18 year olds doing cartwheels in the hallway. Yes, this was the potential director and his assistant. They were playing poker during the downtime and doing cartwheels in lieu of poker chips. They took me in early, handed me a scene to read cold (without any preparation). And then attempted to improvise a scene with me, with them having clearly NO experience in improvisation at all. I will never forget this audition. This was a good example of everything you should NOT do at an audition.

Either in the ad, or at the audition, give actors a time line of shoot/rehearsal/callbacks, and when they should expect to hear from you. And stick to it. Don't waste time auditioning actors that will be away during your shoot dates because no one ever told them when it would be.

What's a "reader"? A reader is someone (another actor, or at least preferably someone with acting experience) who will read the roles in the scene that the actor is NOT auditioning for. Example: It's a 4 person scene, 3 men, 1 woman. An actress comes in auditioning for the woman's role. Your reader would read the other 3 parts in the scene. It's preferable to have chosen audition scenes that only have 1 or 2 characters so that the person auditioning and the reader don't get confused. But also so that you can see how the actor relates to the 1 other person in a scene, instead of spending their energy just trying to keep all the characters straight. A reader's job is NOT to act. Their job is to give a solid, clear, read of the other character(s) so that the auditioning actor can choose to take the scene where they'd like to go. If the reader leads the scene too much, you'll again get 20 actors auditioning the same way.

I had an audition for a student film. It was a very emotional scene and I was supposed to burst into tears after another character goes on a German-accented attack on me. It was going to require a good reader and my listening skills (along with preparation on my part). A friend of mine auditioned for the same part earlier in the day. She didn't have a reader at all.

The director, unfamiliar with the script, read with her. She complained that they needed a reader. By the time I got to the audition, they had a reader. However, in the middle of this rant at me, he stopped, giggled, said he can't do a German accent, said some gibberish, and said, "just go on". You expect me to burst into tears after that? Out of nowhere? I told them, not as nicely as I could have, how to run an audition. I got called back. Go figure.

What's a "monitor"? Your monitor is your go-between. They are your liaison between you and the actors. They'll greet the actors as they arrive. Don't make the actors wonder if they're in the right place. Make it obvious and welcoming. The monitor will organize the waiting area, feed information to the actors, keep the auditions on schedule, inform you of arrivals/late comers, perhaps introduce each actor as they come in to the audition room. The monitor will gather the headshots, give out sides, etc. That saves you from having to do it yourself. A good reader can also double as a monitor.

Why should you videotape the auditions? If you're casting a film, you'll probably want to videotape the audition. You'll want to see how the actor looks on camera, if they're comfortable, know how to relate to the camera, and if they're photogenic. It will also help you accurately remember each actor you see. You can run the camera yourself, but it's best to have someone else (perhaps the monitor) running the camera. Be sure to prepare 2 charged batteries, several blank tapes, a tripod, and a good working knowledge of the camera. You may ask each actor to "Slate" at the start of their audition. To "Slate" is to say their name and any other information you find important (contact information usually). Slating is one way to keep organized, but you can also keep headshots in order of the tape so that actors don't have to Slate.

DURING

You want to have a sign in sheet. It can be as basic as the actor's name and phone number. But you may also want their email, their appointment time, what role they're being seen for.

I also suggest having an information sheet to give to the actors saying when your film will be rehearsing and shooting, and a list of names of who's in the audition room. It may be helpful to write a very brief synopsis of the film to have on hand at auditions. I suggest having an audition form for the actor to fill out with these questions (samples):

1. How'd you hear about the audition
2. Schedule conflicts
3. Full contact information

4.   Reasons you'd like to do the project.

Again, it's important to have rented a quiet,

clean, professional space. It ensures a professional aura

and fewer disruptions during the audition.

When the actor walks in your room, please

welcome them. Shake hands or introduce yourself.

Give them your undivided attention. This is very

important. Please don't eat/talk on the phone/write

notes to each other during their audition. This was the

number 1 pet peeve of the actors I polled. Have some

professional courtesy. Acknowledge their entry and

pay attention.

I suggest talking to the actor for a moment

before you start. Just say hello, comment on their

resume or outfit, anything to break the ice. Ask them if

they have any questions before they start. Double check what side or monologue they will be doing and let them proceed first without any direction. You want to see what dramatic choices the actor has made first.

It's important to not give too much information first, because you want to see what the actor will do with just the material given. If an actor makes you laugh on a line that you've heard 10 times already, then give them the part. If an actor makes you cry, makes you hear a line you've never noticed before, etc. Give them the part. If you give the same background and direction to every actor BEFORE they read, then you'll get 20 actors reading the part the same way. You'll have no surprises and it'll be hard to cast. Be sure and ask the actor if they have any questions or anything else they'd like to say or do. Let them feel like they did all they could at the audition.

If their read is horribly wrong, but you see potential, THEN give them an adjustment (more on that later). If they did fine, you may still want to give a direction just to see if they can adjust and how they take it. And/or have them read another scene/monologue. Again, give an adjustment.

The idea behind giving direction at an audition is:

1. to see if the actor and you communicate

2. To see if the actor can take direction and adjust

3. To see if the actor will do the role the way you envision it (or better)

4. To see if the actor will treat you with respect.

Therefore there are 2 ways to give direction.

1-give an adjustment that may or may not be right for the final production, just to see what change the actor can make.

2- give an adjustment to guide the actor in the direction you do want, to see if they're right for the role.

These are not mutually exclusive. Example: An actor comes in and reads a scene just perfectly. You can't imagine it being better. But you still want to give them direction to see how they handle it. Don't assume every scene will be perfect every time. Try something completely different, just to try it.

Regarding giving direction: Like I said, every actor is different (just like people). Some actors want to discover things in their own way, and some are perfectly happy to have you tell them exactly what you want. Sometimes, YOU don't know what you want, you just know it isn't what they're doing. Maybe you want it angrier, louder, sexier, or more tender. Maybe the actor is playing the scene to seduce, to provoke, to manipulate, or to torture, but you want it played like they're trying to frighten the other character. Whatever it is, say it. If you know what you want (other than demonstrating how you want a line to sound) and the actor knows you know but aren't telling them, that's condescending and actors hate that. You can always ask an actor how they like getting direction. They'll tell you. But to start every direction with "that was great, But…". That's treating them like children. Be clear, be strong, and they'll gladly follow you. They're happy to be lead by a strong leader. They want the director to be the Captain of this ship. They don't want to think that they're about to take a ride at sea with no one at the helm. Otherwise, you get a mutiny.

If you realize after they've read the scene, that there is some pertinent information about the character that they obviously don't know and that that information will help them, then now's the time to tell them. Example: they JUST broke up with their boyfriend/their mom just died/they just got walked in on by someone. Or- this scene takes place in bed/in prison/while drunk. What you DON'T have to say is a whole history of the play and character. This wastes a lot of time and may only confuse the actor. You want to give direction that will change how the scene is played NOW.

If you have (and I hope you have) already given the actors a synopsis of the piece, please don't reiterate it during the audition. You only want to give new information that will inform their performance/ create a new direction to their interpretation. IE: You've already said how old the character is, what the story line is, and who the characters are in the scene. Don't tell the actor this again. They will be racking their brain to figure out if you're saying something different than they already know. Tell them something that will change what they just did in the reading. Something they don't already know. Example: what happened JUST before this scene, what happens just after the scene, what the character's feeling/thinking that might not be obvious.

Only have one person (the director preferably) give direction at an audition (or ever, especially at rehearsals). Getting direction from 2 or more people is only confusing, frustrating, degrading, and possibly conflicting.

Actors like getting direction. It means they're worth trying it again. They know it means you want to see if they take direction. They appreciate it. But give 1 or 2 clear, simple directions and give them a second to process the information. Don't give too much information. If they're completely on the wrong track, you can and should stop them. Don't waste your time. Don't let them be bad. An actor making a daring choice is one thing, a completely wrong choice is another. That's when it's important to give direction and see if it changes their performance.

You want each actor to read at least 2 scenes. You want to see a range of emotions or levels. You want to give them direction/changes. See how they react to you. Can you communicate with them? Do they seem nice, responsible, and pleasant to work with? It's important, so don't minimalize that.

Remember, you don't need to decide right then. In fact, you shouldn't. Take time to see who you remember. Review the videotape. Schedule callbacks as an option. Read several people together. Do they have chemistry? Do they look different from each other? Or look like they could be related? Did they show up on time for the call backs? Don't give callbacks on the spot. And don't give them in front of another actor. Please wait for the audition to be over, gather your thoughts, evaluate time considerations for callbacks, and then call the actors. There is nothing more discombobulating than hearing someone else get a callback right next to you, especially if they read for the same role you're about to. You won't get a good audition out of the next person and it'll create a divisive atmosphere in the waiting room. Keep a "maybe" pile of headshots. Keep a pile of headshots of people you love, but are wrong for the project. You never know when you will need actors again.

Be sure and let the actors know when they'll hear from you. Actors know if they don't hear at all, they didn't get it. But give them a timeline, don't let them wait. And if you have the ability to call/email actors who didn't get cast, please do so as a courtesy. It'll be very much appreciated and remembered for future auditions.

I once had to go WAY out of my way (out of town) to get to a callback for a film. I inconvenienced a friend and myself to get to this callback. When I arrived, the crew wasn't ready. In fact, I had to wait about an hour for them to be set up. Just before reading the scene, I was told by the director that his producer insisted he have callbacks, but that I'd really already been cast. This was a terrible time to tell me. I was extremely annoyed at his wasting my and other's time. And now I don't know what to do for the scene. The audition had been a month before. What did I do? What if I blew it and now the director realizes he made a mistake and yet, he already told me I'd been cast!? Crazy. Plus, when the scene was done, the director said we were going to do it a bunch of times, do voice looping, and do improvisation. That would have taken hours and I was NOT going to do it. I did get the film, I did do the film, and they were HORRIBLY unorganized and ran WAY over schedule. Like I said, the audition sets the tone for the whole production. Their initial audition was run beautifully, or I would not have gone to callbacks at all.

Is the script better than you remember? When the actor comes in and it sounds funnier, more interesting, more touching, you know you've found the right actor.

And lastly, be kind. They are doing their best, just like you. You need them to be good and they want you to be good too. They took time off of work/school/life to be there, so show them some appreciation. It'll go a long way.

AFTER

OK. You've had auditions. You've maybe had callbacks too. You're ready to call and offer a part. That's great. Have all your ducks in a row before you call: schedule, role offered, financials, perks, etc. gather as much information as you may need. They may need a day or 2 to think about it and you want them to have all the information. When you call, please sound enthusiastic and grateful. You are excited to work with them and it's going to be a positive experience for them. You will guide them, take care of them, and have an excellent end product. You should be prepared with second choices of cast just in case you are turned down, or schedule conflicts arise. Therefore, make offers first to actors who are most important on the list. Example: You're casting a father and son. It's easy to cast the dad, you have several wonderful men. It's harder to cast the son. Your first choice for the son is tall, blond, with blue eyes. If he accepts the role, you want DAD #1, with a similar look. If your first SON choice turns down the role, then your second choice is a short redhead. The DAD would be choice #2. Etc.

Above all else, be kind, treat them with respect. Be genuine and caring.

I suggest keeping headshots/reels of actors you'd like to work with in the future. Let them know they weren't right for this project, but that you're holding onto their info.

First day of rehearsal- have a complete contact sheet of all cast and crew. This is vital. Start on time. Set a precedent.

A WORD ON OTHER TYPES OF AUDTIONS

There are of course scores of other types of auditions: plays, musical theater, industrial video, sketch comedy, stand up, commercial, circus act, etc. Since I'm focusing on student film auditions I'll say very little about other types. Plays are pretty much the same process.

However, I did hear from actors that begged me to tell you:

When holding musical auditions, please:

1.   Use a good accompanist. It's just painful to sing with someone who's piano playing is working against you instead of with

you. And you'll never figure out if the singer
can sing.

2.   For singing auditions, ask for
contrasting selections, songs that show range,
preferably the same type as the music or
character. Just as you would for scenes or
monologues.

INDEX

A PARTIAL LIST OF PLACES TO LIST AUDITIONS:

Websites:

IMDBpro.com

Actorslife.com

Backstage.com

Mandy.com

Castingnewyork.com (NY only)

Nowcasting.com

Sagindie.com (for SAG films only)

ActorsAccess.com

LACasting.com (Los Angeles only)

castingconnection.com

thebuzznyc.com (NY only)

castingaudition.com/auditions.com

Hollywoodauditions.com

Nycastings.com

search the internet for other places locally

Other:

your school bulletin board

local acting school bulletin board

Contributors:

Sean Harris

Robin Segal

Cat Parker

Virginia Roncetti

Cecelia Frontero

Heather Morris

Ben Alexander

Tim Sutton

Debra Whitfield

Mirra Bank

Kari Swenson Riely

Ishai Setton

Paul Obedzinski

Marion Kummel

Jonathan Zuck (back cover photo)

Friends

CPSIA information can be obtained
at www.ICGtesting.com
Printed in the USA
BVOW08s0757231017
498396BV00002B/194/P

9 780615 146898